# WILLOW HAMMER

Also by Patrick Donnelly

*Little-Known Operas*
*Jesus Said*
*Nocturnes of the Brothel of Ruin*
*The Charge*

Translations with Stephen D. Miller

*The Wind from Vulture Peak: The Buddhification
of Japanese* Waka *in the Heian Period*

# WILLOW HAMMER

## Patrick Donnelly

*Four Way Books*
*Tribeca*

Library of Congress Cataloging-in-Publication Data

Names: Donnelly, Patrick, 1956- author.
Title: Willow hammer / Patrick Donnelly.
Description: [New York] : Four Way Books, 2025.
Identifiers: LCCN 2024035159 (print) | LCCN 2024035160 (ebook) | ISBN
9781961897304 (trade paperback) | ISBN 9781961897311 (ebook)
Subjects: LCGFT: Poetry.
Classification: LCC PS3604.O5634 W55 2025  (print) | LCC PS3604.O5634
(ebook) | DDC 811/.6--dc23/eng/20240802
LC record available at https://lccn.loc.gov/2024035159
LC ebook record available at https://lccn.loc.gov/2024035160

This book is manufactured in the United States of America and printed on
acid-free paper.

Four Way Books is a not-for-profit literary press. We are grateful for the assistance
we receive from individual donors, public arts agencies, and private foundations
including the New York State Council on the Arts, a state agency.

We are a proud member of the Community of Literary Magazines and Presses.

# CONTENTS

—

*invisible processions*

—

Notes & Acknowledgments

for the willow

*leaving the pleasure district*

he disappeared under the arcades,
among the shadows and the evening lights,
going toward the quarter that lives
only at night, with orgies and debauchery,
with every kind of intoxication and desire

— Cavafy

Byrd *Mass for Four Voices*

on the radio, and Christ it's the 80s again,
and after a whole night at the baths, I'm a baritone
in the back row of a choir ten blocks west.
A *professional*, fresh from the conservatory.

Bathhouse and parish both named for saints:
I paid to enter the house of Mark, who ran away
naked when Jesus was arrested, and where
I wrestled all night, though not with angels.

Then, 9 a.m. in the house of Joseph, God's cuckold,
I was paid in turn—the church *paid* me—
to be another man, of the 1580s, who opened
his practiced mouth with a clear, untroubled tone.

Two wrestling saints, lowest of the four voices—
once I thought I saw them kiss each other's faces.

## About a Year before My Father Left

my mother demanded to know
why I'd written on my sheets in blue ballpoint.

With my allowance, she said, I'd go myself
and buy another sheet, with a high thread count.

A mystery, the writing was in French.
Nobody I knew spoke French, though

I'd always thought it would be exciting
to be observed speaking in French,

answering the telephone for instance. *Oui allo?*
*Les grands jets d'eau sveltes parmi les marbres—*

when can you deliver the great slender fountains
between the marbles? I require them *tout de suite.*

I didn't remember having written in French,
and nobody raised the question of who else might

have access. Once I woke to find a bricklayer
sitting on the edge of my bed. It's true

I'd followed him around the yard a day earlier,
helping him mix his cement. But I don't want to spoil

*this* sheet—writing a memory instead of a mystery.
Suppose I did write it.

Maybe a person can copy a text from the future
without being able to understand it—

maybe live unhappily, not even believing
in happiness at all, while bearing inside a secret

language of romance, maybe a whole nation
of wine and light and perfume.

## How Was I Supposed to Grow Up Straight

when already at ten I knew the Latin
for *the son is the husband of his mother*?
How many midnights did my mother load
the LP of *Oedipus Rex*, lower the needle,
Stravinsky himself conducting for her,
for her racoon eyes and her benzos, as she leaned
alone, mercy, mercy, onto the loveseat
in her corduroy caftan covered with strawberries—

# When You Go to Venice Alone

you'll haunt the narrow corridors at night,
circling the blackened palaces.
Long after the market has closed, cobbles
strewn with mint and crushed flowers,
you'll watch a waiter lower the umbrellas,
stack the chairs and hose the pavement.
And when *he* finally appears,
about twenty and no English,
you'll shadow him past the Fenice,
follow his gesture up the endless stairs.
At first you won't see his old parents
on the couch, lit by an American gameshow,
and when you finally reach his tiny room
at the top of the house—each waiting
for the other to confirm *why we are here*—
you'll do nothing but sit on the narrow bed
and smoke, exiling your homeless blue breaths.

# On the Metaphor "Writ in Water"

The old temple, the eastern hills,
the forest, almost no visitors,
thatched gate, raked sand blurred
by rain, mossy stones, carved
footprints of the Buddha: all that
familiar for anybody who knew
that place.

        But here's a new thing:
a pointed leaf rested on the lip
of a copper basin, held by a pebble,
water trickling over like a thread.
Who made that? How long
would it last? I want to say
something about *Art*,

                but now
I'm remembering a guy who
drank a slender stream from
my dick in the alley behind
the Bijou Cinema Triple-X.
Married, kids, investment banker,
for years came to me in Brooklyn,
a long trip from the east side,
until I asked to meet in a diner,
told him I'd read a book

that said I needed "to create
an empty space for something
better." He looked sad, said *OK*
while shaking his head *no*.
For a long time I thought
I'd been a fool to throw away
what little I had.
                    The water arcs
off the leaf, a drink for
a sparrow in the gravel.
I think I'd been trying
to leave my mark
with my dick. All my life,
like a kid peeing
his name in snow.

# The Uses of Pain

When they wheel us from surgery
we feel none, but as we begin to stir
they ask us to rate our pain one to ten,
and wrap us in sheets from the warming cabinet.
Green clogs and shower caps move around,
asking Where is the key to the narc closet?
A dad offers a graham cracker to a boy's lips, saying
If I was the one hurt, wouldn't you feed me?
A woman refuses to give her pain
a number, only more, less, better, worse.

I beat a man once with my fists and belt,
for his pleasure and mine, each of us
certain the other was paying attention.
Picture us afterward, poor and tender
as swaddled saints, and shriven clean,
like when one has wept for a long time.

If anyone had tried to offer us *love*
we would have carried it in our mouths
to the nearest dung hill, and let it fall.

# Dirk McDermott

Fellow Scout who could climb and touch
the gold ball at the top of the flagpole,
and do math three grades ahead
under his crewcut. I need a calculator
to figure how long since I spoke his name.
How long since I offered my own blue
neckerchief to wipe his always runny nose.
But last night in smoke, steam, and rain
beside a wrecked train I told him
how happy I felt in the igloo we'd built,
how handsome a cub he'd been crawling
on all fours up the twilit tunnel to me.
In a hoarse whisper and never looking at his face.

# Syrinx

We drove straight through, Ohio to New Mexico.

Him at the wheel, me in the back.

23 hours straight, with stops to piss.

I picked him up at the conservatory, where he played the flute.

Me at the wheel, him in the back.

Playing Debussy's "Syrinx" from memory.

Unlike absolute music, this music told a story.

Gas station Cokes, gas station pissoirs of the 70s.

Where we looked straight ahead, not aside at each other.

The story, maybe one wanted it, maybe the other didn't.

Winter, a time of year when people visit their families.

He picked me up at the conservatory, where I was a singer.

I asked if he knew "Syrinx," to show I knew what's what.

When I was in back, I didn't sing him anything.

Can't remember his name. I can't call up his face.

What would I have sung, to show I knew what's what.

Don't look up Syrinx: it's the usual Ovid shitshow.

I wouldn't have sung anything about the great god Pan

or her hiding in the reeds his breath blew through.

We drove straight through. We never touched each other.

# Travelogue

When the wind crosses Nebraska,
there's an éclat to the hip-deep grasses, food
of creatures who took birth to become meat.

A cornflower I picked in a parking lot
in Kearney wilted at the neck
forty miles from its own dirt.

We have to pay close attention
to keep the long truck above the speed
that makes us shake.

On a blue and white cup packed in the back
a windmill reflects in the river, a man drives his
sheep through the gorse. Belonged to your mom.

Everything is in the truck. Your parents and mine.
The road built for us by those who
bombed the rock to make the rough places plain.

And now the way is plain, and straight,
and dangerous, and boring.
Marcus Aurelius said consider

that animals are buried in the bodies
of those who feed upon them.
I thought, then we're our mamas' graves,

out here cruising the highways?
An emperor might envy how we
can push a button at the rest stop

to hear about the weather ahead.
We've lived for three days with only
a cooler full of tea and bread.

Could I live in Iowa, you ask, if a job
for you came open there?
Crossing the Mississippi in rain,

watching for signs, we talked about
what we would do if we were young,
and I said *yes we should do it.*

*scenes from latin poetry*


*Qui tacet consentire videtur.* Silence gives consent.

*Veritas odium parit.* Truth creates hatred.

Willow flower

You know how you can know some things

but forget you know until it's time to remember.

Mom met her third husband Billy when

she was a teacher helping convicts get their GEDs,

and he was incarcerated at that prison.

When he was paroled, they wed in the backyard

with the petunias. Plighted their troth,

as they said, while I sang a song, lyrics

from the Song of Solomon. *A garden inclosed*

*is my sister, a spring shut up, a fountain sealed.*

And then Mom brought this Billy person

into the house with my actual sister, who at fourteen

was skinny as a willow in flower.

Eight years older, I was far away, gone, useless,

just the three of them in that house.

Billy had looks and strength, a crewcut and a drawl.

And my sister was a teenage votress of chaste Diana,

goddess of a whole moon of not wanting it.

Billy chased her, and as in all the old stories, she ran.

*O swear not by the moon, the inconstant moon!*

But my sister *was* constant, she constantly didn't want

his goat breath on her neck. She'd rather die,

and after that she would try, several times.

Later, Billy said it didn't happen (a thing the gods

always say), and Mom said *if* it happened

my sister should have run faster or changed into a tree.

Later, Mom said she never said this, would never

say such a thing, said they were both drinking,

said she didn't know, said about herself that she was

a terrible, terrible mother, inviting us to contradict her.

My sister didn't tell me for twenty years. I didn't know.

That year I had been at a seminary (for fuck's sake),

chaste votary of pale Jesus, while my sister ran away,

lived on the street, and I didn't know, didn't hear

when Mom and Billy broke up. And when he went

back to prison for holding up a Circle K I was

mopping the marble chapel and studying Latin,

*Da mihi multa basia, mea bella puella!* translating

Catullus for a test, *da*, imperative case, he

commanded the girl to give him hundreds of kisses.

So many, a bewildering number, to shake everyone

into confusion. No jealous person could touch him,

because no one would ever know the true number.

## After forty years

Having excluded the word "rape"
from a certain poem, I asked myself,
*Do I know anyone who has been raped?*

It took me a moment.

## Correction

Poets have mistaken the opening
at the end of the cock for an eye.

It's a mouth, that forces
other mouths to kiss it.

It's a grave, the door
to Hadrian's bulbous tomb

at the edge of the Tiber.
A palace, a garden, a prison.

The cock begs to be buried
in a mossy scabbard, just as

the angel sheathed his sword
to signal the plague was over.

Billy,


a boy's name, like "Billy the Kid."
Diminutive of William, Germanic,
meaning "helmet of desire."

The word بلی,
("billi") in Urdu,

means puss, pussy, pussycat,
shaft, and *preventer*.

People want to forget that

the names of God include

the delayer, the subduer,
the compeller, the distresser,

constrictor, humiliator, abaser,
avenger, the taker of life.

Baby, I've seen angels drive the wind.

In which I consider an etymology


Willow flowers, called "catkins,"
appear in early spring before the leaves.

From Middle Dutch *katteken*, meaning "kitten."

Female catkins consist of a single one-celled ovary,
and a small, flat nectar gland.

# The Tale of Murasaki

Genji had been away for an undetermined while.
But one night while Muraskai's mom was cashiering
at the truck stop, 7-to-11, Genji came back
to the house where Murasaki was alone.
He peered through the blinds, circling the house,
pounding on the doors and windows, howling
*I only married your mother to get sex with you.*
Certain he'd break in, Murasaki fled out the back
and hid in the scented hollow of a juniper, until
Genji reached in and pulled her out by her hair.
Juniper, from Latin, is compounded from roots
meaning "to create" and "youth." *Evergreen.*
The tree's tiny fleshy cones, crushed and mixed
with alcohol, will cause a fetus to abort.

A correspondence


The Taira empress leapt into the sea,

after putting her warming stone and ink-stone inside her kimono.
Using a rake, the enemy pulled her out of the water by her hair.


I gripped my sister
and brushed her hair hard.
On a certain day,
when we were alone.


Mom would leave the hospital.
When she returned to the house,

when the key turned in the door,

every hair on our heads
would be perfect, numbered, known.

When my sister and I talk now

it's to compare what we can't remember.

For instance, each other.
Where was the other in the house
all those years.

Where was she on the day, etc.
Where was I when.

Where was everyone.

In the translation my husband and I made,

Jakuzen's spring poem #6 asks, "if the willow / gives itself to the flood / how can the wave break it?"

In prose he added, "Although the water of a great river can tear the various grasses and trees, the willow doesn't break as it surrenders. And although the great flood of birth and death can cause ordinary people to wash away and drown, the bodhisattva has a soft and flexible heart, that won't be reborn, won't circle through birth and death."

"Thus is it written."

*Optimi natatores saepius submerguntur*

The best swimmers often drown.

## Could the poem be in English

I remember a poet friend asking
in response to one of my obscurities.

But consider, this speaker may be trying
to cajole the reader to ask what kind of person,

in what state of mind, retreats from English,
or rather blurts some English out,

then runs away, unable to stay in a relationship
with other people's pain, in the vulgar

language common to them all.
This is because there's a monkish room beckoning

to him from the 12th century, where he might talk
to himself about various things he's read.

There, the light is latticed, and after he's read
the poem in Provençal, he might close his eyes and rest.

Don't pretend your comforts are more defensible.
Don't pretend your weakness is easier to forgive.

Billy's tattoos


Naked girl in a martini glass.

A peacock, covering some older obscenity.

Clipper ship in full sail.

Cherries.

Biceps, shin, chest, ass.


He walked around in his boxers a lot.

When my sister was 14, Mom told her

sex with Billy was the best of her life.

# The Cloak and Dagger Tattoo website

says traditional ship tattoos symbolize "new journeys/beginnings, home, good luck, a way of life, direction, bravery, honor or even a troubled past."

The martini girl was captioned "Man's Ruin."

Darwin wrote of the peacock, "The sexual struggle is of two kinds; in the one it is between individuals of the same sex, generally the males, in order to drive away or kill their rivals, the females remaining passive; whilst in the other, the struggle is likewise between the individuals of the same sex, in order to excite or charm those of the opposite sex, generally the females, which no longer remain passive, but select the more agreeable partners."

But let's talk about

those cherries on his ass.

Let's talk about

how my heart fluttered up
the two or three times
I ever saw him.

## Addendum

When willowy, unrequited, polygonal Lytton Strachey was asked

"What would you do if a Hun tried to rape your sister,"

he answered,

*I would attempt to interpose my own body.*

## A species of fruit fly

I read that it's difficult to
keep cherry trees alive.
The larvae of *Rhagoletis cerasi*,
with yellow legs and green eyes
having red reflections,
feed on the flesh of the cherry
until exiting via a small hole,
which in turn is the entry point
for an infection after rainfall.

In the dream of cherries,
from my high seat in the branches
I eat them warm from the tree.

# I try Google

but the specific crimes of anyone incarcerated
before the 1990s are hidden from my cursor.
I'd have to travel to the archive,
sit in a dark room with a microfiche.

"Billy Chester Hall," 0 results.

*Show yourself, you devil.*

## Show yourself

Every night before bed
the monks at Gethsemani Abbey in Kentucky
turned to face a stained glass window
showing the Virgin Mary shooting milk
from her breast
                          into
the mouth of St. Bernard—

(the word *metaphor* comes
from Greek and Proto-Indo-European roots
meaning "over, across," + "to carry," and also
"to bear children")—

and then the monks sang at her
*Monstra te esse matrem.*
"Show yourself to be a mother,"
imperative case. A command not to prove
virginity—Mary was already famous
as a *hortus conclusus*, a garden enclosed—

but maternity.

But how does a person prove they're a mother.

*

If you think about it,

St. Bernard must have opened his mouth.

Planned Parenthood


invented FRIES, a memory model for consent:

>Freely given
>Reversible
>Informed
>Enthusiastic
>Specific

Which must seem unforgiveable to a person

who longs above all things

to forget.

Some versions

say the Virgin's milk hit St. Bernard
in the eyes, causing him to see things
that had been hidden from other men.

# A few nights later something white

splashed in my face
as I turned in bed:

the moon through a
gap in the drape.

One month she's
at the North window,

next month in the East.
Her hard virgin light

circling the world,
reminding people

someone might be watching
and writing everything down,

unlikely as that seems.
If you ask the monks

at Gethsemani why
they pray in the middle

of the night, they say
that's when men

do most of the things
for which they'll need

forgiveness. *Men,*
they say, specifically.

## The etymology

of the Latin root *matr*
means that *mother, material, matrix* and even *matter*
are sisters.

But doesn't *monstra,* verb imperative insisting "show (it)"
sound too much like *monster*?
"Person of inhuman cruelty or wickedness,"
usage traced to the 1550s.

And in fact, the link between "proving"
and "object of dread" is
demonstrable.

I didn't consent to wanting
to look, so

monster, *don't show yourself.*
Keep Billy ye gods hidden

in whatever world
he now inhabits. Because

what kind of dangerous would he still be,
if I found him? To me, I mean.

In life, he had a gun.
At this distance

can he hold a gun to my mind?
Wizards make a hand sign for *AVERT*

that looks from a distance like a gun—
point at the thing you want to fuck completely off

with index and middle fingers together,
thumb and other fingers circled underneath

and Pop! away it goes.

Only, did that ever work. In what world.

# Riddle

In Syriac, my sister's name means the moon.
In Sanskrit, essence, main point, substance.
Among the top given names since 1880.
Half-sister to her own husband,
according to the Book of Genesis.
Beginning in January 1939, the Nazis forced
female Jews without "typically Jewish" names
to add my sister's name to theirs.
Mom hated her own middle name,
said she hated middle names for girls, if asked
told people my sister's middle name was "Period."
As in, given-name-plus-family-name, *period*.
What is her name. Say it. Say her name.

How do you prove harmlessness

It's possible there's still
a violent smear of Billy's atoms
somewhere on the world.

If I were a wizard,
would it be better to bind him
or disperse him.

## Alexander the Great

once dragged the Oracle of Delphi
out of the shrine by her hair, more or less

because the people at the front desk
said they were closed that day.

Outside, she said something to him,
and he replied, something something—

which all got written down because
they thought it might be important.

Even this late in history,
some weirdo's parsing the text,

assigning numerical values to the awful letters,
attempting to make the stories add up

to something different from what
the god already said must happen.

Last car

My sister, born 10.4.1964, Santa Fe, NM. Not dead.

Billy Chester Hall, born 1939. 83 now, or dead.

Subtract 1939 from 1964. That's an order, it's imperative.

Mom, born 3.14.1928, Summit, NJ, died 5.5.2005, Las Cruces, NM.

Smoked for sixty years, those brown More menthols.

Married Billy, divorced him, married him again.

Her last car was a 1989 Buick Skylark. This book tells the rest.

Received wisdom


When I say: in summer I lower the shades
on the east side of the house in the morning,
and the west side in the afternoon,
Mom says:
You learned that from me.

When I say: my sister's acted quickly
to give order to chaos at her house,
Mom says:
She had a good example for that.
I never let chaos reign.




Or did I.

Questionnaire

Asked why he didn't protect my sister from Billy,
our real dad said, "Everybody goes through hard things.

That's just life. I shot somebody in Korea."

Should there be a statute of limitations?


When critic William Logan called Franz Wright's poems

"the crude, unprocessed sewage of suffering" and suggested that
"after forty years there should be a statute of limitation..."

Wright replied, "I do not wish to kill you or hurt you, and so I beg
you to get away from me, without delay, if you realize we are in the
same room somewhere."

Delicate, the qualifications, the contingencies, *do not, without delay,
if, somewhere.*

The first line


of Catullus 16 tells two of his critics

*I will butt-fuck and face-fuck you.*

Lines two through thirteen lay out

a detailed argument, which concludes

*I will butt-fuck and face-fuck you.*

My husband said, I don't believe you.

When I showed him proof, he said,

This is not how I expected to begin the day.

## The backs and the outsides

Billy told me to do the dishes again,
because I hadn't washed
the backs of the plates
and the outsides of the bowls.

He was right, something I face
each time I stand at the sink.

Sometimes I think of saying what Billy said to me
to my husband, who also doesn't wash
the backs of the plates
or the outsides of the bowls.

But I can't say it. I can't make my mouth.

Here is a curated list of rapes in Ovid

Alcyone. Turned into a kingfisher.

Anaxarete. Turned into stone.

Arethusa. Turned into a lake.

Callisto. Turned into a bear, then some stars.

Cyane. Dissolved into a pool of tears.

Daphne. Turned into a tree.

Dryope. A tree.

Io. A cow.

Leucothoe.

Nyctimene.

Syrinx.

Frankincense, hoot owl, hollow reeds that rattle

in the wind.

Rattle-tittle-tattle when people

are trying to rest! Why dredge up the past? For once

can't we just have some peace and quiet.

It was Jia Tolentino who said

I think a lot of people in this world have turned into a tree and then turned back again.

For instance, my sister, who in the more recent past


gave our real Dad many more chances than I.
Visited, bothered to cry when he died.

Took care of our Mom at the end.
Left her first husband twice before the final time.

Had her nails painted with sunflowers
for her second wedding, which also didn't take.

Now her first ex takes care of the dog Hannah
during the week when she's busy with school.

Which makes her two adult kids angry, because if
they don't hate each other what was the point

of the divorce? Teaches with a body mic, because
the thyroid surgeon screwed up her voice,

sometimes forgets to turn it off in the bathroom,
comes back to find fifth graders giggling at the sound

of flushing, funniest of all the world's infinite sounds.
Walked so far down the long corridors between

portable classrooms that she cured her diabetes.
Joked about day drinking when six of her class

came down with Covid, including the boy who always
had to sit right next to her because he pulls the girls' hair.

Sunflower, *Helianthus annus*, exhibits heliotropism
(symbol of adoration) in the young flower stage only.

Citalopram and gabapentin for depression.
Named the gray kitten Cenizas,

                              Spanish for "Ashes."

# Sequelae

There were the years
my sister's first husband
decided he didn't want his kids
around gay, viral me.

There were the years
I said to them all
if you come to town,
I'll leave the town.

If you ascend into heaven,
I'll make my bed in hell—

# In which I appoint myself dramaturge

This time the Billy character
is paroled onto an oil platform

in the middle of the Gulf,
overflown by a lone brown pelican.

Mom never met Billy,
never had the best sex of her life.

Christ never had to save me.
I never had to believe in any holy pelican

who would tear its own breast open
before it would let its brood go hungry.

# The Three-Body Problem in physics

has no general solution.
No one can predict their
actions relative to each other.

To my students, I say try
several elements
in the position of the main thing before deciding—

the Moon, the Earth, the Sun—

then keep one hand on the main thing
when speaking about each of the lesser things.
We might call it the Mother Hand.

The atmospheres around us can be sweet,
full of color and intensity. But what if

we're still sentenced to orbit some cold giant
we never seem to glimpse or forgive

or admit we long for and adore?

## Palindrome

Finally, like and unlike

that girl who begged
any elemental that would listen
to thicken her body
so the god wouldn't chase her anymore

every day this year my body
grew grosser and more rank.

No god will ever wear what I leave
in his hair.

In his hair,
no god will ever wear what I leave.

My body, every day. This year
grew grosser and more rank.

So the god wouldn't chase her anymore,
her body thickened:
any elemental would have listened
when that girl begged.

Like and unlike, finally.

*Ilico*

*Germanae meminī salicis vitreae fuit instar*

*Cui imposuit manus malleolis saevis.*

Now

I remember my

little sister that was,

little willow of glass

upon whom he laid

his hammer hands.

*invisible processions*

When suddenly, at midnight, you hear
an invisible procession going by
with exquisite music, voices,
don't mourn your luck that's failing now,
work gone wrong, your plans
all proving deceptive—don't mourn them uselessly.

— Cavafy

# Spell Check Corrects HIV to VIP

Which is
a little bit funny,

and even possible,
if each of the dead

were welcomed,
crowned,
compensated.

Or does it mean

there's a place where
AIDS
never happened,

where
*hawk* (never)
*caught the dove*

*or the swift hunter*
*the hare in fields*
*of snow*

— after Horace

## Willow Song Sampling

Mrs. Danvers, will you brush my hair
100 strokes, as of yore?
Eeyore, Eeyore,

your garlands rich with bees
will be the end of me.
Io, Io,

her hide stung by flies
across the wide Levant.
Next stop

Esopus, Esopus.
Please take your refuge with you.
My eyes itch—Emilia,

put this ring away. Put these
flowers in the attic.
How quickly

everything dies, the meadow
in its brindled coat!
What's that sound? Just a

lonesome whip-
poor-
will, my lady.

A willow grows aslant the brook,
where waly, waly
I reached my finger

into
some
soft bush.

I'm sleepy—
shall I lie in your lap, Camerado,
and let the oozy weeds about me twist?

The dead man touch'd me from the past.
Well, he is dead, and where shall I find another?
It takes years to train a man to love me.

# Vigil

When a man asks "Do you think I made him happy?"
about another man who will live maybe three more hours,
and you are the only other person in that room, no sound
except the wide city of children shouting and cars passing,
and the long night still to get through, the correct answer,
the answer you will wish you had given, is *Yes*.

# Buick Skylark with Alcoholic

My mother was poor, on welfare at the end,
but still imperial to her home health aides.
They were "getting fatter every day,"
and stupider, not remembering where
the last fucking silver forks belonged.
She said she'd read "everything" forty years ago,
Malory, Browning, Eliot, Unamuno,
and then she said she'd forgotten it all.
Richard Strauss is all sex and no orgasm,
she said to me when I was ten years old.
Many nights she said mix my scotch,
then till 4 a.m. stacked records on the hi-fi,
Stravinsky, Stan Freberg, "The Sound Of Silence."
In grad school she translated "The Wanderer"
better than the *Oxford Companion to English Lit.*
She never said that. I said it, after she was gone,
to myself. She got the alliterative tetrameter,
mid-line caesuras, the Norse mind, everything.
She sold her old Skylark with the peeling leather
to her aide Carmen for a dollar, every detail
of that transaction illegal. *But joy is a ghost.*
*Hopes may hover        but fail to flower.*
One Christmas I borrowed that car back,
and because of Carmen's many DUIs had to blow

into its breathalyzer to start it, then blow again
when it died in the middle of the intersection.
Everyone in that little desert town judging me,
innocent princeling, for a poor woman's crime.

# Sciatica

Panicking in the MRI canal sciatic jolts swarming
me I almost made them end it only the shame
of needing to start over kept me from pressing
the bulb the technician said was super-sensitive
I wanted to shout *don't forget me* a mistake to ask
for the local classical station the pounding
began they had warned me about Schubert
String Quintet in C major interrupted by the
composer's death but then came the screech that
always precedes an emergency warning a flood
in the northern counties *don't drive into water that*
*may seem shallow wait on your roof for help to arrive*
I tried to do what the old texts advise hold
holy faces in mind the words of certain prayers
but no god could unroughen my passage because
I saw for the first time the flood and my mind
of endless disappointment felt *good* to one another
and for a moment I was happy now I could change
I could judge more skillfully but how ghastly
that the past need not have been so sad insight
like the sudden tragic downwash *oh there I've*
*done it again* rescue helicopter

               hovering directly over my skull.

# The Enthusiasms of Innocence

Innocence is indeed a kind of insanity,
my love, an affliction disguised by charm.

At the conservatory in my twenties, I knew
Peter G., a combined piano and cannabis major
who carried the whole mind of adolescence
into his adulthood. At the end of every day
his cheek wore a five o'clock shadow.
But he was still a boy, who could sing all
the patter songs from Gilbert & Sullivan
*in Yiddish*, and would and did and did.
His mouth twisted with any musical exertion—
little rascal making the difficult marble shot—
and in winter he wore a bath towel
for a scarf. From mailing tubes
and duct tape he built all the instruments
needed to perform a satire of Bach,
and taught himself to play them,
the "Windbreaker,"
the "Left-handed Sewer Flute,"
the "Lasso d'Amore," and we laughed until
we were sick. But after a time, Peter began
to shoot from behind his thick black
horn-rims looks of longing toward

a girl who played the viola. When
nothing came of it, which the innocent don't
yet understand is the default outcome,
it seemed he almost came to hate her,
and to hate desire itself, which had no place
in the life of a boy. In his towel he trudged
the streets, muttering *Willow, titwillow.*

In late spring there's a moment the wind
fingers the blossoms, and then they should fall:

the enthusiasms of innocence were lies.
I said, I can't be with a man

who hasn't accepted falling.
Your eyes, my love, opened a long time ago,

in all of the five ways. Someday
even the grasses and trees will open their eyes.

# Garden, 1964

To hang in a hammock of Spanish lace vine
and eat sour cherries from the warm branch.
To let the pits fall.
In a bowl, to grind the hard orange berries of mountain ash
and mix the paste with water from the hose,
dyeing strips of cloth and drying them
to see what color they'd turn out.
The smell of mother in the house making jam
out of our pears, too sticky and sweet,
but the wish to hold the cool flesh of one pear
now against my forehead.

The long *canales* that emptied rain from the roof
into a stone gutter that circled the house, then ran
into the street like a brook.
When there was no rain, to run the hose
and pretend it was my own river working
through the thicket of lilac, white blight
on their summer leather.
To talk to myself about things I had read.
To help Hutch the handyman carry the bucket,
mix cement in the wheelbarrow,
sit with him while he rolled a cigarette.
Bonnie the border collie following him too

as he laid the bricks so cement oozed out between the rows.
For decoration, he said,
the cement petals hardening and for years
breaking off a little at a time.
To wake one Saturday,
the war we supported escalating,
to find Hutch sitting on my bed
in the basement room he built for me.
He had even dug a hole for a window
so I could have light down there.
Leaning into my side, whispering, entreating.
The upper world muted and still,
father at work and mother asleep.
Overhead,
mint in the pebbles where the spigot dripped.

I have a fever as I remember this,
the same age now that he was then.
I think I might have loved him.
I think I can sleep now.

# Four Waters

*One*

In winter, water comes cold
from the hot tap until I count
                              thirteen.

*Two*

The cows at Siaconset had a pox and
bearded Ben had to rub their teats with paste.

              Thirteen, I drank spring water

from a grassy pool the Pilgrims knew
and the woods were full of ferns and fog.

Dorothy and Tom divorcing in the dry west
sent me to the wet east, the mist, the island,

to live with actors, summer stock, a mercy.
Ben played Henry in *The Lion In Winter*,

told me my Dad remarried fast because
he was not the kind to whore around,

showed me how to cook a meal
without a recipe: some tomato,

some fennel, improvising like Coltrane.
Barbara with the long red braid

picked berries on the moor,
made me a most tender cake.

I stole somebody's skiff, Pyewacket
or some such, abandoned it to the reeds

when I couldn't row it back.
Loved Birdy, a golden retriever,

loved my role, Robbart, speaking
Welsh in *The Corn Is Green*,

loved a younger boy in the barn
who wasn't that into it.

The summer gone, freak snow
over the ocean, a little plane

carried me away.

*Three*

A muscly guy I met on the Super Chief
Chicago to Albuquerque asked if he could
sail his boat up the Santa Fe River
to visit me, and did I want to count his tattoos?
My answers were *no*, because in autumn
the river runs dry (water drawn off
into the *acequias* for the corn), and *yes*—
turned out there were
                          thirteen, all homemade.
It may have been a dry bed then,
but now in my memory the water's fat
and noisy. The foam has a cold tang
and overshoots the mossy banks.

*Four*

Young players and singers, not even graduated from Oberlin, Juilliard, Curtis, Peabody, we were hired to wait tables and play Mozart. After the guests went to bed we swam in the lake, but was it thirteen fathoms, the summer water, or thirty or three hundred, when a line of storms came across? That summer a woman I knew wanted to visit and talk with me about God. Guests were forbidden, but I said come anyway. We hid her in the staff cabin, fed her cold lobster stolen from the walk-in. Somehow every afternoon she strolled down to the beach and spread her blanket.

One night the soprano who played Fiordiligi, talking to somebody else, poured boiling water onto my hand at the sink. Three of us piled into a station wagon to take me to the rural ER, an hour away. It was August 6, 1978, which I know because Pope Paul VI died that day. We drove through the closed-up woods, in and out of the fog—until suddenly a sheet of flame fell onto the road in front of the car. The driver, a guy I loved on the maintenance crew, jammed the brakes and we looked at the road and each other. The flame was gone, but we all agreed we saw it. Probably only I thought of the pope.

We drove on until we arrived at the two-room clinic, where a handsome doctor began to work on my hand—until an alarm rang, a woman in an ambulance, pills, overdose, etc. They put me in the hall with my hand in a bucket of ice and Ruth the French Horn player held my other hand. After a while I heard the woman ask for a cigarette. They bandaged my fist like a football, sent me back with a week of Demerol.

The next night we sang *Soave sia il vento*
in a glass pavilion on the lake,

my burn aching. We never learned

anything more about where the fire fell from,
or how deep it had hidden, or when

it might rise to the surface again.

Notes & Acknowledgments

The epigraphs for the first and third sections of the book are from, respectively, Constantin Cavafy's "One of Their Gods" and "The God Abandons Anthony," from *C.P. Cavafy: Collected Poems*, translated by Edmund Keeley and Philip Sherrard. Copyright 1992 by Edmund Keeley and Philip Sherrard. Reprinted by permission of Princeton University Press via Copyright Clearance Center.

"On the Metaphor 'Writ in Water'": John Keats asked for the phrase "Here Lies One whose name was writ in Water" to be inscribed on his grave in Rome. In 1817 he wrote to Benjamin Bailey: "…if a sparrow come before my window, I take part in its existence and pick about the gravel."

"About a Year before My Father Left": "Les grands jets d'eau sveltes parmi les marbres" is from Paul Verlaine's "Clair de lune."

"Syrinx": in Ovid, a chaste nymph whom the god Pan attempted to rape was transformed into water reeds by her fellow nymphs, which Pan cut to make a wind instrument. Virtually every flutist is expected to know Debussy's 1913 "Syrinx," a short piece for solo flute.

Scenes from Latin Poetry:

Epigraphs: "Silence gives consent," attributed by some to Thomas More (1478–1535). "Truth creates hatred," attributed to Terence (Publius

Terentius Afer, 195/185–159 BCE).

"Willow Flower": The poem refers to Catullus 5, *Vivamus, mea Lesbia, atque amemus.*

"Correction": in Rome, the statue of an angel on the roof of the Castel Sant'angelo ("Hadrian's bulbous tomb") commemorates the end of the plague in 590 CE.

"People want to forget that": the names for God in the poem are among the "99 Beautiful Names" (or attributes) of God in Islam.

"The Tale of Murasaki": in medieval Japanese culture, women spent much of their lives cloistered behind screens; for a man to catch a glimpse of a woman was intensely eroticized in art and literature. The act of a man spying on a woman was so common (as depicted in *The Tale of Genji* and elsewhere) that it had a specific name, *kaimami*, "peering through a gap in the fence."

"A correspondence": the account of the Taira empress's attempted suicide is from the 14th c. Japanese epic *The Tale of the Heike.*

"*Optimi natatores saepius submerguntur*": "The best swimmers often drown." Possibly unattributed; recorded by Hendrik Dominicus Suringar in 1873.

"The Cloak and Dagger Tattoo website": the Darwin quote is from *The*

*Descent of Man and Selection in Relation to Sex*, 1871.

"Addendum": Lytton Strachey (1880–1932) was a queer pacifist; his quote is a sly jab at assumptions about war and heterosexuality. Strachey's biographer, Stanford Patrick Rosenbaum, referred to one of Strachey's many romantic entanglements as "[a] polygonal ménage…"

"Show yourself": the stained glass window the poem describes is one of many artistic depictions of "The Lactation of St. Bernard"; *Monstra te esse matrem* is a passage from the Ave Maris Stella prayer.

"The first line": the translation of the first and last lines of Catullus 16 is mine. Because Latin had quite specific names for sexual acts, the meaning of these lines has been perfectly clear since antiquity, though translators often euphemized them with clinical or abstract language.

"It was Jia Tolentino who said": the quote is from "The Brutality of Ovid: A conversation on sex, violence, and power in the *Metamorphoses*," by Stephanie Carter and Jia Tolentino, Lapham's Quarterly, 2019. https://www.laphamsquarterly.org/roundtable/brutality-ovid

"Sequelae": the title is a medical term, meaning conditions which are the consequence of a previous disease or injury. The last two lines allude to Psalm 139: 8 KJV, "If I ascend into heaven, You are there; If I make my bed in hell, behold, You are there."

"In which I appoint myself dramaturge": it was an erroneous medieval

Christian belief that in the absence of any other food, pelicans would wound their breast and feed their young with their own blood. In the hymn "Adoro te devote," St. Thomas Aquinas described Jesus as the "good pelican" whose blood saves the world.

"The Three-Body Problem in physics": physics, classical mechanics, and Quantum mechanics have tried to model the chaotic, non-repeating interaction between three bodies, or three particles.

The Latin version of my poem "Now/I remember," which appears as a grey ghost at the end of "Scenes from Latin Poetry," was written by Stephen C. Farrand. Latin poetry was invariably metrical, so Stephen's poem is not only a translation of my poem, but an actual Latin poem. I'm very grateful for his collaboration. Here is his note on the translation:

"I chose the elegiac distich meter (also called elegiac couplets) because of its history and status in the classical world. Elegiac distichs, like all surviving Latin classical meters, are originally Greek. It is thought to have been first used in Ionia for songs of mourning. But already in the 7th century BCE, the Parian poet Archilochus used it for lyrical expression on a range of subjects. By Hellenistic times its use had expanded to love epigram, narrative and didactic poetry. The Romans used it for epigram and love poems, although Ovid re-expanded its purview to didactic and narrative poems."

"Spell Check Corrects HIV to VIP": the italicized lines were translated by Ellen Bryant Voigt from the Roman poet Horace (Quintus Horatius Flaccus, 65 BCE–8 BCE), specifically his ode "Nunc est bibendum" (Odes, Book One, Poem 37).

"Willow Song Sampling": A little like the "cento" poetic form, except that my sampling includes passages and connective tissue that I wrote myself. My sources: Mrs. Danvers, Daphne du Maurier, *Rebecca*; Eeyore, A.A. Milne, *Winnie-the-Pooh*; in Ovid's *Metamophoses*, Io was one of many women Zeus raped and ruined; Esopus is a town in upstate New York; *Flowers in the Attic*, 1979 novel by V.C. Andrews (subsequently a play and movie); "How quickly everything dies…the meadow in its brindled coat," Charles Grandmougin (1850–1930), from "Adieu," set to music by Gabriel Fauré, translation mine; "My eyes itch—Emilia, put this ring away./What's that sound," Shakespeare, Othello, Act 4, scene 3; "lonesome whippoorwill," "I'm So Lonesome I Could Cry," Hank Williams, 1949; "A willow grows aslant the brook," Shakespeare, *Hamlet*, Act 4, scene 7; "waly, waly I reached my finger into some soft bush," from "O Waly, Waly," the Scottish folk song; "Shall I lay in your lap, Camerado?" mash up of Hamlet to Ophelia and Walt Whitman; "I'm sleepy, and the oozy weeds about me twist," Herman Melville, "Billy in the Darbies"; "The dead man touch'd me from the past," Tennyson, "In Memoriam"; "Well, he is dead, and where shall I find another? It takes years to train a man to love me," Katisha, from *The Mikado*.

"Four Waters": maybe a variation on a *haibun*, as the first section is a *haiku*, and the last section is partly in prose. The sections correspond to the four seasons, and the word "thirteen" appears in each section. No matter how old I get, when I think of the age I feel inside, it's always about thirteen.

I'm deeply thankful to the poets who advised me about these poems, including Doug Anderson, Melanie Braverman, Maudelle Driskell, and Henry Israeli. Heartfelt thanks too, to Laurel Blossom, Maury Cohen, Martha Collins, Paul Lisicky, Randall Mann, and Diane Seuss.

George Bealer and Keith Gresham, cherished friends.

To everyone at Four Way Books, especially Martha Rhodes, Ryan Murphy, Hannah Matheson, and Sally Ball, my gratitude for all that you do.

Always my first reader, Stephen Miller: *you, to teach me.*

I'm grateful to the editors of the journals and websites in which these poems previously appeared: *Academy of American Poets Poem-a-Day, The Adroit Journal, American Poetry Review, The Georgia Review, The Iowa Review, The Los Angeles Review, On the Seawall, Poetry Northwest, Under a Warm Green Linden, upstreet.*

PATRICK DONNELLY is the author of five books of poetry. Former poet laureate of Northampton, Massachusetts, Donnelly is program director of The Frost Place, a center for poetry and the arts at Robert Frost's old homestead in Franconia, New Hampshire. His poems have appeared in *American Poetry Review, The Georgia Review, The Iowa Review, The Massachusetts Review, Ploughshares, Slate, The Virginia Quarterly Review, The Yale Review,* and many other journals. Donnelly's translations with Stephen D. Miller of classical Japanese poetry were awarded the 2015-2016 Japan-U.S. Friendship Commission Prize for the Translation of Japanese Literature. Donnelly's other awards include a U.S./Japan Creative Artists Program Award, an Artist Fellowship from the Massachusetts Cultural Council, and an Amy Clampitt Residency Award.

WE ARE ALSO GRATEFUL TO THOSE INDIVIDUALS WHO PARTICIPATED IN OUR BUILD A BOOK PROGRAM. THEY ARE:

Anonymous (14), Robert Abrams, Debra Allbery, Nancy Allen, Michael Ansara, Kathy Aponick, Jean Ball, Sally Ball, Jill Bialosky, Sophie Cabot Black, Laurel Blossom, Tommye Blount, Karen and David Blumenthal, Jonathan Blunk, Lee Briccetti, Jane Martha Brox, Mary Lou Buschi, Anthony Cappo, Carla and Steven Carlson, Robin Rosen Chang, Liza Charlesworth, Peter Coyote, Elinor Cramer, Kwame Dawes, Michael Anna de Armas, Brian Komei Dempster, Renko and Stuart Dempster, Matthew DeNichilo, Rosalynde Vas Dias, Patrick Donnelly, Charles R. Douthat, Lynn Emanuel, Blas Falconer, Laura Fjeld, Carolyn Forché, Helen Fremont and Donna Thagard, Debra Gitterman, Dorothy Tapper Goldman, Alison Granucci, Elizabeth T. Gray Jr., Naomi Guttman and Jonathan Mead, Jeffrey Harrison, KT Herr, Carlie Hoffman, Melissa Hotchkiss, Thomas and Autumn Howard, Catherine Hoyser, Elizabeth Jackson, Linda Susan Jackson, Jessica Jacobs, Deborah Jonas-Walsh, Jennifer Just, Voki Kalfayan, Maeve Kinkead, Victoria Korth, David Lee and Jamila Trindle, Rodney Terich Leonard, Howard Levy, Owen Lewis and Susan Ennis, Eve Linn, Matthew Lippman, Ralph and Mary Ann Lowen, Maja Lukic, Neal Lulofs, Anthony Lyons, Ricardo Alberto Maldonado, Trish Marshall, Donna Masini, Deborah McAlister, Carol Moldaw, Michael and Nancy Murphy, Kimberly Nunes, Matthew Olzmann and Vievee Francis, Veronica Patterson, Patrick Phillips, Robert Pinsky, Megan Pinto, Kevin Prufer, Anna Duke Reach, Paula Rhodes, Yoana Setzer, James Shalek, Soraya Shalforoosh, Peggy Shinner, Joan Silber, Jane Simon, Debra Spark, Donna Spruijt-Metz, Arlene Stang, Page Hill Starzinger, Catherine Stearns, Yerra Sugarman, Arthur Sze, Laurence Tancredi, Marjorie and Lew Tesser, Peter Turchi, Connie Voisine, Susan Walton, Martha Webster and Robert Fuentes, Calvin Wei, Allison Benis White, Lauren Yaffe, and Rolf Yngve.